Instant Microsoft Forefront UAG Mobile Configuration Starter

Everything you need to get started with UAG and its features for mobile devices

Fabrizio Volpe

BIRMINGHAM - MUMBAI

Instant Microsoft Forefront UAG Mobile Configuration Starter

First published: January 2013

Production Reference: 1210113

Published by Packt Publishing Ltd.
Livery Place
35 Livery Street
Birmingham B3 2PB, UK.

ISBN 978-1-84968-878-9

www.packtpub.com

Credits

Author

Fabrizio Volpe

Reviewer

Rainier Amara

Acquisition Editor

Edward Gordon

Commissioning Editor

Yogesh Dalvi

Technical Editors

Jalasha D'costa

Charmaine Pereira

Copy Editor

Laxmi Subramanian

Project Coordinator

Amigya Khurana

Proofreader

Maria Gould

Production Coordinator

Aparna Bhagat

Cover Work

Aparna Bhagat

Cover Image

Conidon Miranda

About the Author

Fabrizio Volpe has worked in the Iccrea Banking Group since 2000, as a network and systems administrator.

Banca Agrileasing (part of the Iccrea Group) was a company with a Windows NT4 and Exchange 5.5 (and Proxy Server v2.0) environment managing 300 users.

Now, as Iccrea Banca in the Microsoft Technologies workgroup, Fabrizio and his colleagues manage more than 2000 users at their central site, a nationwide branch offices network, and provides services for more than 400 banks.

Since 2011, he has been awarded MVP for Directory Services from Microsoft and is focusing on Windows systems and security, unified communication, and virtualization.

Prior to the Iccrea Group, Fabrizio has collaborated with various IT companies, focused on Windows, security, networking, and messaging/unified communication products.

Since 2000, Fabrizio has presented in quite a few events and conferences, online and live (Italian and international ones).

Fabrizio is committed to creating content that is accessible to a wide number of people, so he frequently publishes content on SlideShare and on his Lync 2013 channel on YouTube.

Until May 2012, Fabrizio collaborated with his fellow MVP, Edoardo Benussi, to moderate Microsoft TechNet Forums (in Italian).

Acknowledgement

I would like to say thank you to my family, my wife Antonella and my child Federico, and to my parents and brother for their support and love. This work, and all the rest, would have been simply impossible without them.

I especially want to thank all the people at Packt Publishing for giving me the opportunity to write this book and for all their great work on the long road from drafting to publishing.

I extend my heartfelt thanks to my friends and my colleagues at Iccrea Banca who have supported my work over the past several years.

About the Reviewer

Rainier Amara is a confirmed IT professional with more than 16 years of specialist experience in the field of information security and remote access. From a young age, Rainier was already renowned for his inquisitive nature and attraction to all things electronic, and by the age of 8, he had already embarked on a journey that would feed his passion for IT.

It was in his early teens that he received his first personal computer, but his professional career took off at the age of 18, when he served in the French National Army as a communications engineer. From there Rainier has traveled the world fulfilling various roles and has not looked back since.

He now works in the Microsoft Forefront EDGE team as a security support escalation engineer, where he is responsible for providing customers and partners with the highest levels of expertise and advisory services on Forefront UAG and DirectAccess.

Outside of work, Rainier spends as much time as he can doing lots of crazy and wonderful things with his wife, three kids, and dogs, and as an avid free rider, you'll also find him tearing around the best downhill tracks in the UK and the Alps.

Who knows what the future holds...

www.packtpub.com

Support files, eBooks, discount offers and more

You might want to visit www.PacktPub.com for support files and downloads related to your book.

Did you know that Packt offers eBook versions of every book published, with PDF and ePub files available? You can upgrade to the eBook version at www.PacktPub.com and as a print book customer, you are entitled to a discount on the eBook copy. Get in touch with us at service@packtpub.com for more details.

At www.PacktPub.com, you can also read a collection of free technical articles, sign up for a range of free newsletters and receive exclusive discounts and offers on Packt books and eBooks.

PacktLib.packtpub.com

Do you need instant solutions to your IT questions? PacktLib is Packt's online digital book library. Here, you can access, read and search across Packt's entire library of books.

Why Subscribe?

+ Fully searchable across every book published by Packt
+ Copy and paste, print and bookmark content
+ On demand and accessible via web browser

Free Access for Packt account holders

If you have an account with Packt at www.PacktPub.com, you can use this to access PacktLib today and view nine entirely free books. Simply use your login credentials for immediate access.

Instant Updates on New Packt Books

Get notified! Find out when new books are published by following @PacktEnterprise on Twitter, or the *Packt Enterprise* Facebook page.

Table of Contents

Instant Microsoft Forefront UAG Mobile Configuration Starter   1

So, what is Microsoft Forefront UAG Mobile?   3

Installation   5
    The four faces of UAG   5
    Planning a successful deployment   5
       Step 1 – What we need   6
       Step 2 – Software that we need to have available   7
       Step 3 – Install Forefront UAG   8
       Step 4 – First configuration of Forefront UAG   13
       Step 5 – Updating Forefront TMG and UAG   19
    Summary   21

Quick start – Publishing SharePoint for mobile devices   22
    Portals, trunks, and applications   22
    HAT and AAM   26
    Publishing SharePoint sites for SharePoint Workspace Mobile   28
       Step 1 – Creating an HTTPS trunk   29
       Step 2 – Publishing SharePoint 2010   36
       Step 3 – Enabling mobile devices   43
    SharePoint Workspace Mobile   49

Top features you need to know about   53
    Most common application publishing scenarios   53
       Publishing Exchange ActiveSync for mobile devices   53
       Publishing Dynamics CRM 2011 for mobile devices   58
       Publishing Lync for mobile devices   59
    Security and customization   60
       UAG portal selection   60
       PIN logon   62
       UAG portal customization   63
       Endpoint detection   64
       A quick word on Network Access Protection (NAP)   65
       UAG authentication and SSO   65

Monitoring, maintaining, and troubleshooting   66
Back up and restore UAG configuration   67
Configuration tasks requiring registry modifications   68
UAG Web Monitor   68
UAG tracing   70
People and places you should get to know   **71**
Official sites   71
Community   71
Blogs   72
Twitter   72

Instant Microsoft Forefront UAG Mobile Configuration Starter

Welcome to *Instant Microsoft Forefront UAG Mobile Configuration Starter*.

In a world where the number of smartphones is expected to reach a billion by 2016, companies are in need of working solutions to extend their enterprise resources to mobile users in a secure and effective way.

UAG is Microsoft's answer to this and offers the following:

- A high level of integration with existing Microsoft environments and solutions
- Out of the box features for mobile devices that are really not to be overlooked

The purpose of the book is to introduce UAG as a solution, dedicated to mobile users, to explain the benefits of the UAG solution and to show the various steps we need to follow in order to deploy a working solution.

This book contains the following sections:

So, what is Microsoft Forefront UAG Mobile? is an introductory chapter, with a high-level overview of UAG and a first look at the features and benefits of the publishing resources for mobile devices using UAG.

Installation teaches us how to deploy UAG and how to configure it for access from mobile devices in a quick, easy, and efficient manner.

Quick start – Publishing SharePoint for mobile devices is dedicated to explaining one basic operation of UAG for mobile devices: the deployment of Microsoft SharePoint Workspace Mobile 2010. The steps we will see here will be used over and over again for publishing applications.

Top features we need to know about explains the three basic tasks of UAG for mobile (mobile portal management, configuration of mobile logons and portals, and publishing for mobile devices). By the end of this section we will be able to configure and modify the access to mobile portals, to manage and configure the logon and credentials required (username and password or PIN), and to publish Exchange ActiveSync (with filtering) and Dynamics CRM applications.

People and places you should get to know will have a collection of documentation references, links, Twitter accounts, forums, and resources to help us use UAG at the maximum level.

So, what is Microsoft Forefront UAG Mobile?

Unified Access Gateway (**UAG**) is a product focused on granting access anywhere and keeping centralized entry points and management methods.

The two main features of UAG are DirectAccess and Publishing.

+ **DirectAccess**: This feature is used to extend our network to external users, connecting to clients outside our network even before the user is logged on, and without using VPN or other traditional solutions

+ **UAG Publishing**: This feature is what we want to look into, because publishing gives us the capability to grant access to our applications and resources to people coming from different locations, and from different devices, using a single web application or a Forefront UAG portal (that consolidates multiple resources in a single gateway)

While opening our resources to a wide variety of end points, we need a strong access control, and UAG includes such mechanisms to check clients, users, and groups for authorization and to apply mandatory policies. With the release of Service Pack 2 (August 2012), UAG is now able to interact with the most recent devices from all the biggest players in the mobile market (Windows Phone 7.5, iOS 5.x on iPad and iPhone, and Android 4.x on tablets and phones) and, as soon as an end point tries to connect to a UAG site, there are different publishing scenarios based on the characteristics of the device in use.

The client device discovery mechanisms of UAG give us what we need to identify and provide the best results to different clients and mobile devices. We have two kinds of portals, the **Premium portal** (the suggested solution for devices with good graphic capabilities) and the **Limited portal** (mainly text-based and a viable solution for older products).

A third kind of portal, that is, the **Regular portal,** is the standard for desktop and laptop computers. As we can see in the following screenshot taken from the gateway management screen, the publishing functions rely on two different kinds of connections from UAG to the servers where the applications really are:

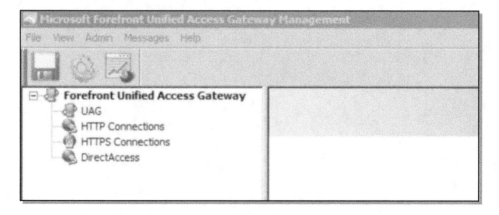

The connections are called trunks and they are available through HTTP or in a more secure HTTPS encryption. The HTTPS publishing used by UAG is an efficient solution for mobile users, both from the point of view of bandwidth consumption and compatibility (the last because the protocol is widely supported on mobile networks while other solutions are prone to various technical issues). The list of what we are able to publish with UAG is rather impressive, including various versions of Exchange, Dynamics CRM, SharePoint, Remote Desktop, and Terminal Services. Terminal Services, applications based on IIS, and on other web servers and client/server applications from different vendors.

Often there is confusion because there is another software that gives us the capability to publish resources, which is the **Threat Management Gateway**. To worsen the situation we have to say that TMG is (also) a part of the UAG setup (with limited function to secure the UAG server from external networks). TMG is an Enterprise Edge Firewall that offers functionalities (from the publishing point of view) that are similar but less powerful than the ones we have with UAG, with limits on what we can publish and on the controls we're able to perform on the connecting clients.

Installation

Installing Microsoft Forefront UAG is a process that can be divided into five steps as described in the following sections.

The four faces of UAG

Microsoft Forefront UAG is a product focused on centralizing and managing access to internal resources from external networks.

The aforementioned statement is expressed through the following four access models:

+ Reverse proxy (portal)
+ Port forwarding
+ SSL VPN
+ DirectAccess

In the course of this book, we will very often use a UAG frontend portal as our central access point to the resources in the backend from mobile devices. We are able to select the HTTP or HTTPS protocol to publish the resources, and the choice will be related to security requirements, with no significant difference in the functionalities available in the two configurations. In UAG, there is also a viable alternative, the capability to pre-authenticate a user account. The access gateway will act as the endpoint of the HTTPS connection and inspect the traffic before passing it to the backend servers for authentication, adding a security layer against common Internet threats.

We are going to explore the previous scenario in the *Quick start* section, because it is one of the methods to configure the Office Hub of Windows Phone to work with SharePoint Workspace Mobile.

Planning a successful deployment

Before installing UAG, there is a planning phase necessary to select the kind of deployment that is more fit to our company's needs. UAG is able to work with different levels of isolation from the internal network and resources that we will make available to external users.

We are able to divide the above aspect into three different design and deployment topics:

+ The logical network in which UAG will be located
+ The security context in which UAG will be working
+ The IT system that will be used for the security, compliance controls, and authorization of the end points that will require access to our resources

Let us start from the first point, the selection of the logical network where UAG will be positioned.

The possible scenarios are as follows:

✦ When UAG is directly connected to an external network

✦ When UAG is behind an external firewall

✦ When UAG is installed in a DMZ between an external and an internal firewall

Our objective is to publish resources in an efficient manner while keeping up the security level. It is a work that requires a balance between control and easiness (often they are inversely proportional). If we plan to connect the external interface of UAG directly to a public network, we are relying on the local installation of TMG with its rules to protect the host. If we have an existing firewall, it's a good idea to keep it in front of UAG, because the level of the security will not be lowered (UAG requires TCP ports 80 and 443, and the HTTP port is in use only if we plan to deploy a listener with no encryption), and we gain an additional layer of security.

The last scenario is a classic DMZ, with a second firewall deployed to isolate the Internet-exposed services from the internal network. The complexity of the configuration will be related to the UAG features we are going to use, for example, with DirectAccess it requires many modifications on the firewall before we are able to make it work. The second topic in our list is the domain membership. We have an easier deployment with UAG added as a member server to our domain, while the reverse scenario (standalone server) is interesting only if we have some concern about security on our UAG server. The third point is the control of the end points as we are able to select UAG or a Microsoft NAP infrastructure to check the devices requiring a connection. We will be talking about this topic later, but using NAP has no benefits with our scenario that is based on mobile devices.

Step 1 – What we need

The minimum hardware requirements are as follows:

✦ 2.66 GHz, Dual core CPU

✦ 4 GB memory and 2.5 GB of free disk space

✦ Two network adapters

There is no official sizing guide for UAG.

A common suggestion is to install a test environment and to evaluate our needs based on this experience.

It makes sense because there are no *typical* deployment scenarios for UAG, and requirements are related to the features we will use and to the number of trunks and applications we are going to use.

The given value for disk space is really an installation minimum. All the user activities will be logged by the system because UAG is also in charge of the application layer security, which implies that we will need a lot of disk space to manage the logs. When the number of connections (or the number of UAG servers) increases, we can send the logs to an external SQL server. The advantages of such a solution are not only related to the disk space and performances on the UAG host, but also to the consolidation and easier reporting of the log data.

Logging to the SQL server requires a configuration in TMG; for more details see the related TechNet article at `http://technet.microsoft.com/en-us/library/dd897065.aspx`.

The following are the software requirements for the installation process:

✦ Windows Server 2008 R2 Standard SP2, Windows Server 2008 R2 Enterprise SP2, or Windows Server 2008 R2 DataCenter SP2.

✦ All the required Windows roles and features will be automatically installed (Network Policy Server, Routing and Remote Access Services, Active Directory Lightweight Directory Services Tools, Web Server (IIS) Tools, Network Load Balancing Tools, and Windows PowerShell).

✦ All the required system components will be automatically installed (Microsoft .NET Framework 3.5 SP1, Windows Web Services API, Windows Update, Microsoft Windows Installer 4.5, SQL Server Express 2005). Forefront TMG is installed as a firewall during the Forefront UAG setup, and following this a Windows Server 2008 R2 DirectAccess component is added.

Step 2 – Software that we need to have available

The most recent version of the UAG installation media (or ISO) has Forefront Unified Access Gateway 2010 with Service Pack 1, and TMG with Service Pack 1 Update 1 slipstreamed. If we select the `setup.exe` file and look at the properties of the file, we will see a product version `4.0.1752.10000`, that is the version number related to the Service Pack 1.

However, on June 8, 2012, UAG Service Pack 2 was released and that is important for our work, because as we said the number of mobile devices supported has been expanded.

The following is the logical order of the installation, using the media available at the time of writing.

The list of the steps is pertinent also for existing installations; we will have to start the checklist from the step following the last applied update.

1. UAG installation.
2. TMG updates (before the UAG updates).
3. TMG SP2 (KB 2555840).
4. TMG SP2 Rollup 2 (KB 2689195).
5. UAG SP1 Update 1 (KB 2585140).
6. UAG SP2 (KB 2710791).

Please remember to activate UAG after any update and before applying the next one. Often there are problems (for example, lost configuration) going from update to update with no activation in between.

If we have already installed UAG and are missing UAG SP 1, we have to install it after updating TMG and prior to step 5 (UAG SP1 Update 1) of the checklist.

Operating system and SQL updates are usually installed before we start with the UAG and TMG updating process, but we are free to apply those updates at the end of the previous steps.

UAG 2010 Service Pack 3 will probably be available during the first quarter of the calendar year 2013, and will provide support for Windows 8, Office 2013 clients, publishing Exchange 2013, and publishing SharePoint 2013.

Step 3 – Install Forefront UAG

It is strongly suggested to use the console for the installation process of UAG.

If we are using RDP, after the first part of the installation process (that includes the installation of TMG) the remote connection will no longer work. We have to modify the TMG rules to resolve the issue. Right-click on **Firewall Policy | All Tasks | System Policy | Edit System Policy**, then go to **Remote Management | Terminal Server | Tab General | Enable | Tab From** and insert the source IP that is allowed to access via RDP to our Forefront machine (for example, add it to **Enterprise Remote Management Computers**).

There are some limits and topics to know before installing UAG. The *Support boundaries* documentation on the TechNet site contains this information. It is available at `http://technet.microsoft.com/en-us/library/ee522953.aspx`.

Setup choices will also depend on the above notes.

1. We can start launching the `Setup.exe` file from the UAG installation folder.

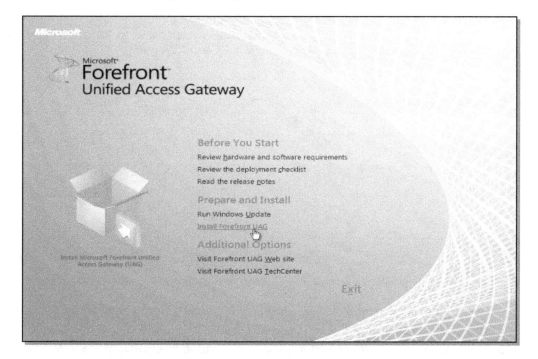

2. We will have a **Welcome** screen, and then proceed using the **Next** button, as shown in the following screenshot:

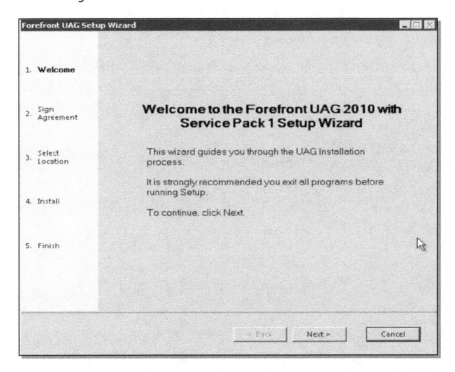

3. In the **Sign Agreement** screen, select to accept the license terms and use the **Next** button.

4. As we previously mentioned in the *So, what is Microsoft Forefront UAG Mobile?* section, the installation process will install a full deployment of TMG and UAG.

   During the **Select Installation Location** screen, we have to select the path where the UAG deployment will be placed.

We are offered no choice on the installation location for TMG.

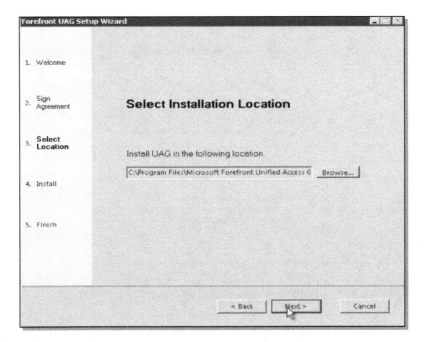

The UAG setup will go on requiring no interaction.

If we are installing with the Windows Firewall active, we will need to permit the Active Directory Lightweight Directory Services Installer traffic.

 AD-LDS will be used by TMG to save the TMG configuration data.

5. After the TMG installation phase, we will be required to restart the server.

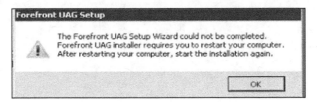

6. The setup wizard will give us the usual radio buttons with **Restart Now** or **Restart Later,** as shown in the following screenshot:

7. UAG installation will continue after we log on again to our host.

8. Another system restart will be required, but this time the message will state that the wizard has been completed, as shown in the following screenshot:

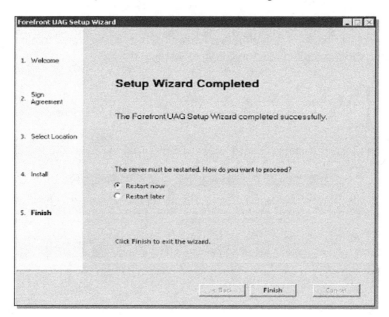

Step 4 – First configuration of Forefront UAG

As we stated in a previous note, it is important to activate UAG before an upgrade with service packs, to prevent installation issues. The very first time we launch the UAG management console, the **Getting Started** wizard will be activated, with the aim to help us in the basic configuration of UAG:

1. At the top of the list, we will have the **Configure Network Settings** procedure.

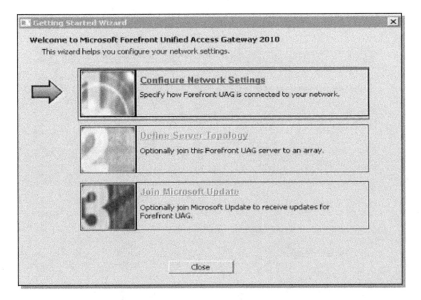

The idea is to help us set the various network interfaces and addresses of our host.

2. The welcome page explains that we will define network adapters and addresses.

3. The next screen will ask us to select the context of the network interfaces we have configured on the host. The main objective here is to define at least an internal and an external network interface.

The only supported configuration is the one with two network interfaces, as is specified in the aforementioned *Support boundaries* document.

A typical configuration requires the *external* network interface configured with a default gateway and no DNS server. The *internal* interface should have no gateway and use the internal network (domain) DNS servers.

If we have an internal network with more than one subnet, this configuration requires us to add static routes to all the networks that are not directly connected to UAG.

This is depicted in the following screenshot:

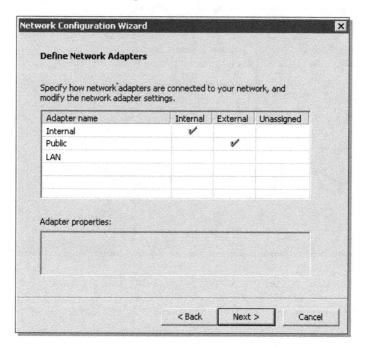

4. The previous step will be followed by the **Define Internal Network IP Address Range** window. As we said, UAG is a software to connect external users to internal resources, so the steps to outline the various networks have a deep impact on all the configurations that we're going to set from now on.

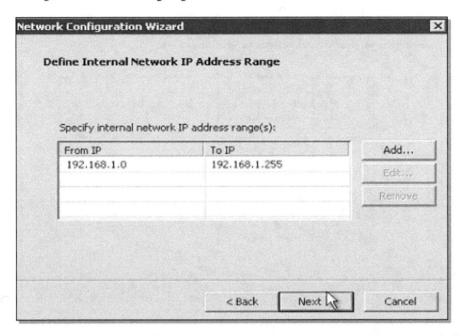

The internal network is configured by selecting the internal adapter. By default, TMG protects the internal network from all other networks except the *Local Host* network. System policy rules in TMG expect services such as DNS servers, RADIUS servers, and domain controllers to be located with in the internal network.

 To learn more, refer to the *Internal and perimeter network properties* document which can be found at http://technet.microsoft.com/en-us/library/cc441726.aspx.

5. We will be asked to confirm what we have done in the previous steps of the **Network Configuration Wizard** window.

6. When the **Configure Network Setting** wizard is completed, we will be moved to the second step, **Define Server Topology**. TMG uses the parameters we have configured in the previous steps to create network objects. For example, our internal IP range is assigned to the internal network object.

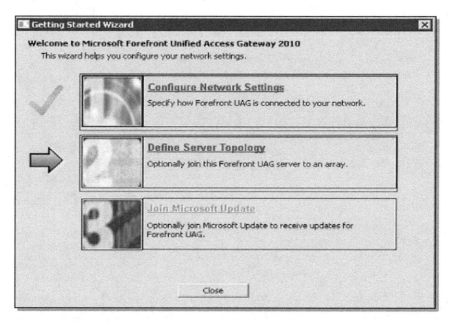

7. The **Server Management Wizard** window is our way to deploy an array of UAG servers or to define a single host. It will start with a simple welcome page.

8. Our configuration will be a single server deployment, so we will have to select the first option.

UAG uses the TMG standalone array infrastructure to provide scalability and high availability. To get started with the installation of a UAG array, we can start from the TechNet article *Array deployment guide* available at http://technet.microsoft.com/en-us/library/dd857305.aspx.

9. A configuration like this requires no further steps, and so we will have a simple confirmation screen.

    We are back to the **Getting Started Wizard** window, with the first two steps cleared, and the last one, **Join Microsoft Update** to be completed:

10. The first screen is a simple welcome screen, so we will go on with the **Next** button.

11. The first decision is related to Microsoft Update; if we want to use it, use our source for updates for UAG (and other Microsoft software).

    TMG also uses the Microsoft Update service to update malware definitions. WSUS is another alternative update method supported by TMG. For a complete table of the available features, refer to the *Configuring update settings* article available at http://technet.microsoft.com/en-us/library/cc995320.aspx.

12. We will have the opportunity to join the Customer Experience Program, so we are able to select our preferred option and the **Next** button again.

13. The wizard is now completed. A last confirmation screen will be displayed and we're able to select the **Finish** button.

14. The **Getting Started Wizard** window will require a last confirmation before activating the UAG configuration.

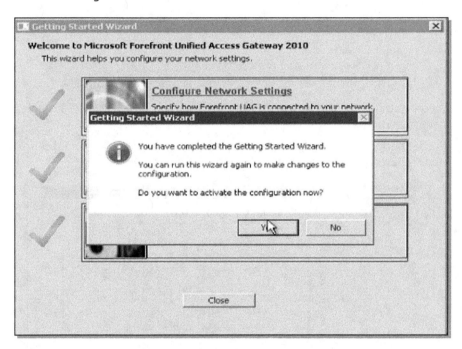

15. Before we activate the configuration, we will be prompted for a path to save a backup of our existing configuration (we can protect it with a password).

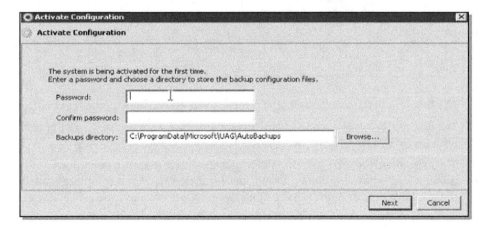

16. A last confirmation to the backup and activation step is required.

 Each time we activate UAG , it automatically exports the configuration (if we leave the checkbox selected). We will talk more about backups in the *Top features you need to know about* section.

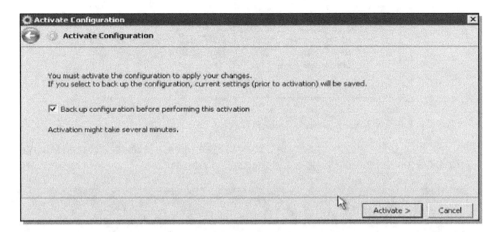

And here we are, the first configuration is completed and we're ready to work with UAG.

Step 5 – Updating Forefront TMG and UAG

We outlined the steps required to upgrade TMG and UAG at the second step of the installation process.

1. We will start our updating process from Service Pack 2 for TMG.

2. The next step is TMG SP2 Rollup 2 (this is cumulative, so we don't need Rollup 1).

3. Now we have to install UAG Update 1.

 If we try to skip the aforementioned update, and go straight to the Service Pack 2 for UAG, the latter will present an error.

4. The UAG Update 1 will start.

5. Now, before we take the next step, it's really important to activate UAG again.

To do so we will have to open the UAG management console and run the little "gear" icon, as shown in the following screenshot:

6. The last step will be the installation of UAG Service Pack 2.

    Again, it's a good idea to check UAG to verify the release level (select the **Help** menu in the UAG management console and then select **About**).

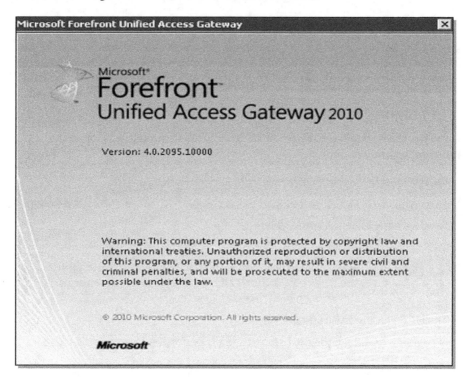

Summary

In the course of this section, we have seen the logic, pre-requirements, and configuration steps required to deploy UAG starting from the installation media and upgrading the system to the latest available service pack. TMG played an important part in the whole explanation because UAG heavily relies on TMG features to deliver its own features. Now with a working installation at our disposal, we will go on to configure SharePoint and SharePoint Workspace through UAG, to learn the fundamentals of application publishing and access.

Quick start – Publishing SharePoint for mobile devices

During the following section, we will take a SharePoint publishing scenario and use it to learn some basic concepts of UAG. The features described here will be used from now on throughout the book.

Portals, trunks, and applications

We said that the meaning of UAG is to publish resources, but it is obvious that at this point in the book we are still working with an empty framework. The only aspect we have partly addressed is security, because during the previous section we installed UAG and now know that TMG is active when it comes to protecting the host. What we now need is a channel to connect the external users to our internal resources, that is what we call a **trunk** in UAG. The configuration of a trunk is an operation that we execute from the UAG management console (as we can see in the following screenshot):

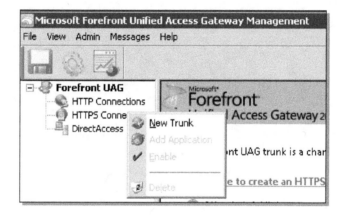

To enable external connections, UAG establishes a listener (an IP address paired with a port), that creates a website in IIS, that will have a name based on the trunk parameters, and a series of rules in TMG (in the following screenshot we can see the result of a UAG portal creation in IIS):

In the following screenshot, we can also see the rules created in TMG which are related to the trunk:

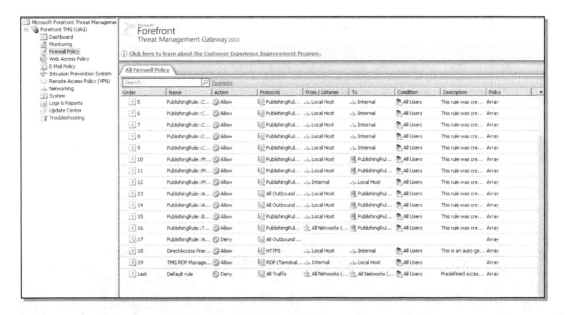

 All of the parameters and settings shown in the previous screenshot are automatically configured, and it is recommended not to interfere in the IIS or TMG parameters without a really good reason.

In UAG, two kinds of trunks are available, namely HTTP and HTTPS. The type of trunk we will select will have a deep impact on the security of our resources, because only when we use an HTTPS trunk are we encrypting the traffic with the end points (HTTP sends all the traffic in clear text).

An HTTPS trunk requires a valid and recognized SSL certificate with a working private key.

 The private key is mandatory for the encryption process, so if we have deleted the certificate request or in a similar scenario, we could try the solution in the TechNet article *Install certificate after deleting the pending certificate request* that is available at `http://technet.microsoft.com/en-us/library/cc759048(v=ws.10).aspx`.

We are free to select a certificate released from an internal certification authority or from a third-party authority. Certificates released from a public certification authority are usually trusted automatically (because the public C.A. certificate is already in the list of accepted C.A.), but if we decide to use an internal certification authority, we have to send the certificate of our internal C.A. to the mobile device. To give an example, we have sent our internal C.A. certificate to an Android device attaching it to a simple e-mail message, saved it on our SD, and we can see, as in the following screenshot, the first step, the **Install from SD card** screen:

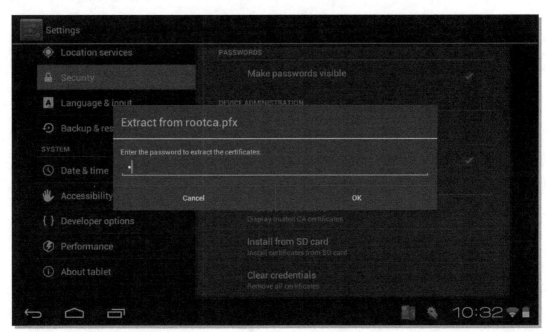

We are required to confirm the import operation as illustrated in the following screenshot:

If we want to verify the previous steps, we can open the **Display trusted CA certificates** screen.

One huge advantage of using HTTPS when we are configuring our trunks is that usually HTTPS encrypted traffic is able to pass through enterprise and personal firewalls while IPSEC or other encryption methods often are not allowed.

Now to make an application available, there is a last step to take — we have to publish it by adding it to a trunk (so we can think of the different trunks in our UAG deployment as folders in which we are able to organize our services).

[Publishing an application is an operation we have to perform (again) in the UAG management console.]

Remote end points can access applications and resources published via a trunk in one of the following two ways:

✦ **Portals**: We are able to create a web portal to act as a gateway for every single trunk. Applications will be published in the portal associated to their trunk.

✦ **Direct connection**: We can publish a web application with a public FQDN, allowing end points to connect directly to the application.

 UAG supports an array of multiple servers and load-balancing on different *nodes* of the array. Each server in the array will make the same trunks available and each trunk will listen to a virtual IP address (VIP) providing scalability and high availability.

In UAG, we have two portals dedicated to mobile devices (in addition to the standard portal used for all the other clients). We have a *Premium* mobile portal for all the smartphones supporting AJAX and pages with numerous graphics files (mobile devices enabled to the Premium portal are the ones running, for example, Windows Phone 7, Windows Mobile, or the Apple iPhone). All the other mobile devices are redirected to the text-based *Non-premium* mobile portal.

HAT and AAM

UAG uses a mechanism called **Host Address Translation** (**HAT**) to publish internal servers with no FQDN resolvable on the external networks. For example, if we have an internal web server, `http://webserver01.internal.intra`, all the contents on that server will use the internal name, blocking the access to Internet clients. Using HAT, UAG takes the URL and replaces the server name with a URL pointing to itself (for example, `http://webserver01.internal.intra/image1.gif` is turned into `http://uag.domain.com/uniquesig2bb49990fd8c6dd09bb3b0f63a3cfb8c/uniquesig0/image1.gif`).

 HAT is the solution we (also) use to unify multiple applications under a single URL.

However, some applications (such as SharePoint) are so complex that the HAT mechanism is not able to correctly replace and modify all the links and scripts. To prevent the aforementioned issue, SharePoint has a feature called **Alternate Access Mappings** (**AAM**) that modifies the URLs before they are sent to UAG. So configuring AAM is a step fundamental to publishing SharePoint in UAG.

To modify the AAM setting with SharePoint 2010, we have to go to **SharePoint 2010 Central Administration | Application Management** as we can see in the following screenshot:

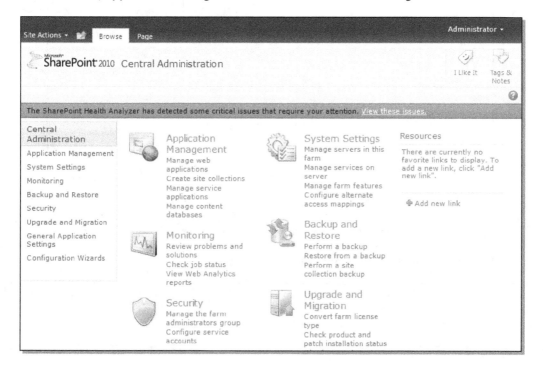

Then we select **Configure alternate access mappings** as shown in the following screenshot:

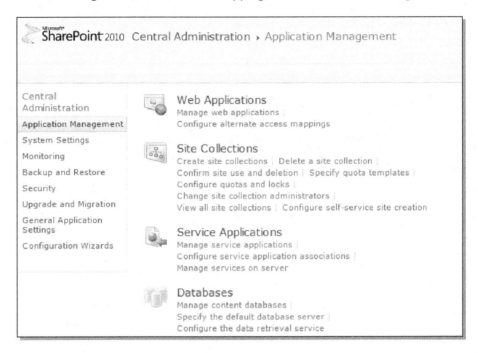

The last operation is to modify the AAM values:

Publishing SharePoint sites for SharePoint Workspace Mobile

Microsoft SharePoint Workspace Mobile 2010 enables smartphones and other mobile devices to edit Microsoft Office documents directly on the mobile device itself. To enable SharePoint Workspace Mobile, we have to first publish a Microsoft SharePoint Server 2010 application through Forefront Unified Access Gateway (UAG).

 We have talked about the need to have an SSL certificate to create an HTTPS trunk (that is the first step of our procedure). We can refer to one of the many articles on the topic, such as http://technet.microsoft.com/en-us/library/ff720335.aspx.

Step 1 – Creating an HTTPS trunk

The most common configuration is the one based on SSL, as all the communication with the end points is secured with encryption.

1. To begin, let's select **HTTPS Connections** in the UAG management console and select **Click here to create an HTTPS trunk,** as shown in the following screenshot:

2. After the wizard starts, we can select the **Next** button and go to **Step 1 - Select Trunk Type**. We will create a portal trunk (exchange publishing not selected, at the moment).

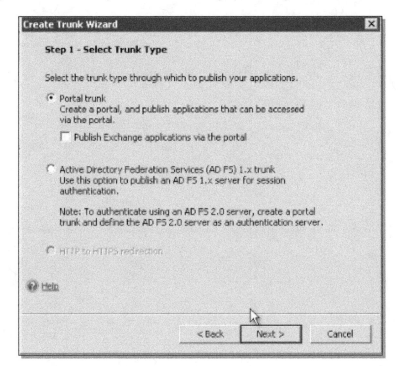

3. In the following step, we will give a name to the trunk and add all the information about the server FQDN, IP addresses, and used ports.

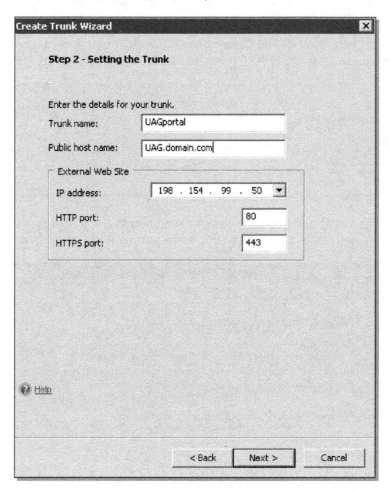

4. The next screen is all about the authentication repository. We will use Active Directory, so we have to select the **Add...** button and select **Add** again in the **Authentication and Authorization Servers** screen.

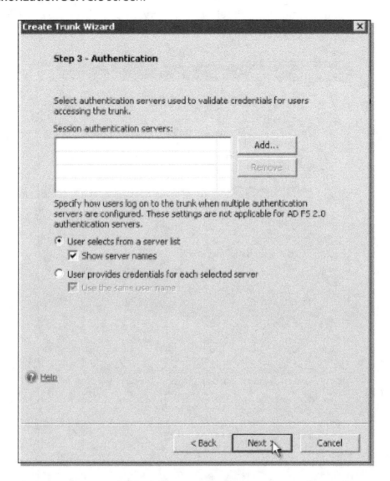

5. If the UAG server is a member server of an Active Directory domain, we can select **Use local Active Directory forest authentication** or else we have to define the domain controllers.

With **Use local Active Directory forest authentication,** any available domain controller in the forest will be used. It is recommended you use this option if the Forefront UAG server's domain joined a forest and we want to authenticate users from that forest.

6. The **Search settings** group is automatically populated the first time we click the ellipsis button, and we can leave them alone if they are set to our directory structure (by default the **User** container is selected).

 We are able to expand the search to subfolders and nested groups, but add these options only if they make sense in our directory environment.

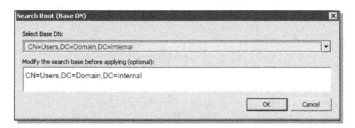

7. The two options still empty are **Server access,** where we have to insert a user enabled to read the A.D. information, and **Default domain name** that is optional but it helps our users gain access in an easier way.

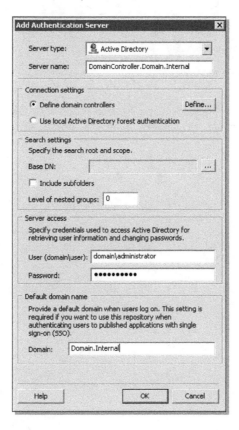

8. Step 4 of the wizard is about the selection of a valid SSL certificate.

9. The following screenshot is about **Endpoint Security**. We will keep the default selection (UAG access policies) with no modification, also in the screen that will follow, which is **Endpoint Policies**:

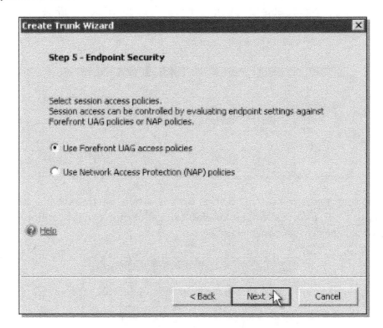

 We will talk again about the selection of UAG or NAP as end point security servers later in the book.

10. The final screen confirms the trunk creation and lists the parameters we have selected during the procedure, as shown in the following screenshot:

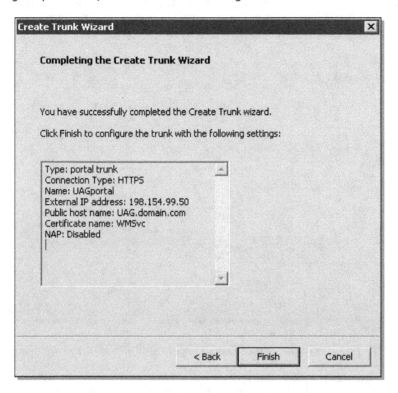

Step 2 – Publishing SharePoint 2010

1.   Back to the UAG management console, we're able to add SharePoint to the applications related to the HTTPS trunk we just defined. Selecting the **Add** button under the applications list, the **Add Application Wizard** will start.

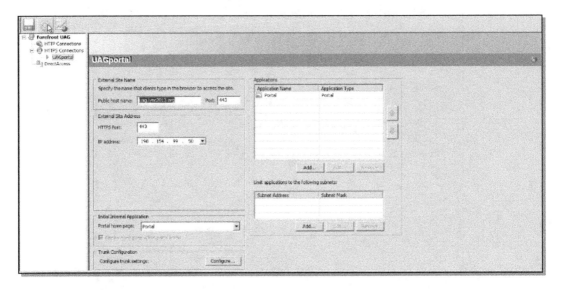

2.   After the first screen, we are enabled to select SharePoint 2010 from the list of web applications:

UAG provides three templates to publish SharePoint sites.

We are going to use Microsoft SharePoint Server 2010 that provides support for the version of AAM we need in our scenario.

3. Step 2 requires a name for the application and in step 3 (**Endpoint Policies**) we can leave the default parameters and click on **Next**.

4. In step 4, we have to select the kind of SharePoint deployment we want to have:

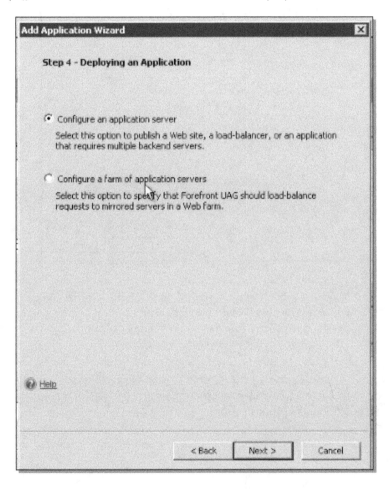

5. The next screen will require information about the SharePoint web services:

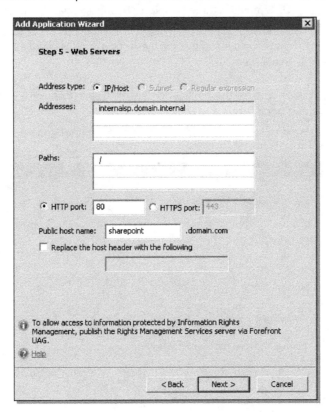

 There are four different scenarios, in which the internal and public names of the SharePoint server could be identical or different. In the previous screenshot, we have an example of a configuration with an internal and a public name that are not the same.

6. In step 6 (**Authentication**), we were able to manage settings such as the single sign-on to multiple applications by credentials delegation (for trunks that use Integrated Windows Authentication).

Another really interesting option is **Allow Rich Clients to Bypass Trunk Authentication**: rich clients can authenticate directly with the SharePoint site's authentication server, and an end user can open documents published on SharePoint directly from the client application, without using the Forefront UAG portal.

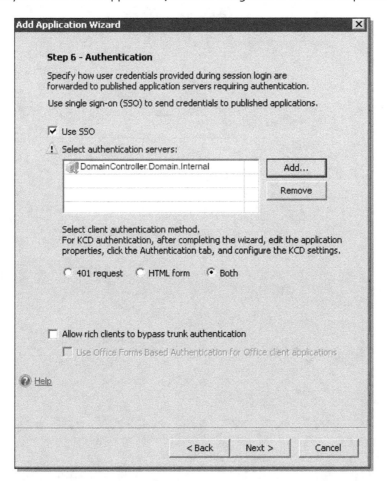

7. We can go on pressing **Next** till **Step 7 - Portal Link**. We have to remember the value of the **Application URL** set in this step because we will use it again in the SharePoint AAM configuration.

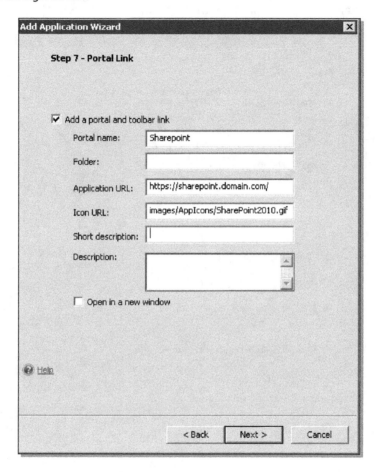

8. The **Authorization** step (step 8), allows the filtering of users and groups, so that SharePoint is available only to selected users.

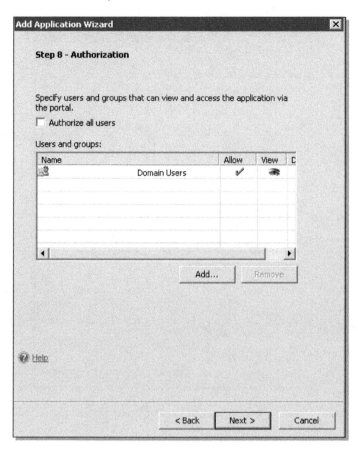

In the **Authorization** step, we are able to configure different repositories to authenticate users. This kind of flexibility allows us to design different scenarios for user authentication and access (in the following screenshot we can see the screen in which we are able to use the various repositories).

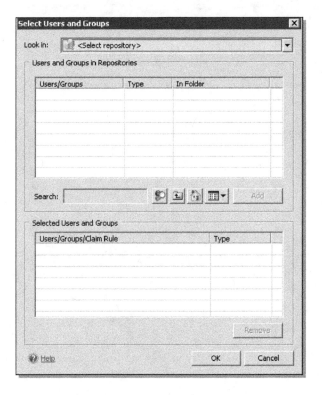

Step 3 – Enabling mobile devices

The steps we have carried out have published SharePoint for a standard client. What we need now is to enable mobile devices to access our application.

1. The first step is to press the **Configure** button in the **Trunk Configuration** zone of the portal:

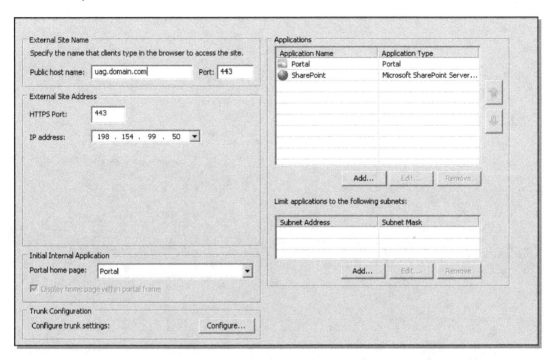

2. We have to select the **Endpoint Access Settings** tab in the next screen that appears and click on **Edit Endpoint Policies**.

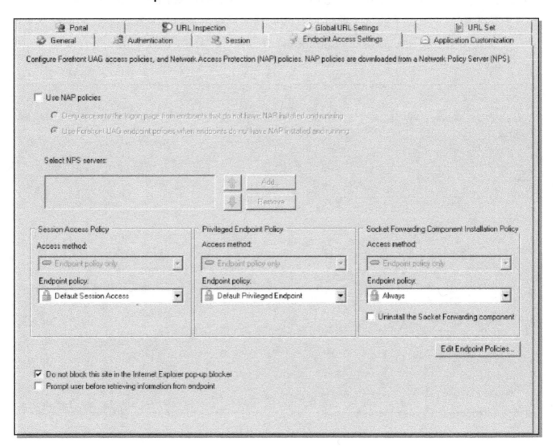

3. We have to edit **Default Session Access Policy** and **Default Web Application Access policy** (using the **Edit Policy** button for each one), as shown in the following screenshot:

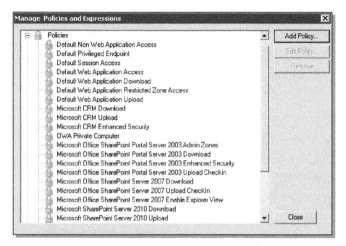

4. In the **Select platform-specific policies** list, select the **Other** drop-down list and click on **Always**.

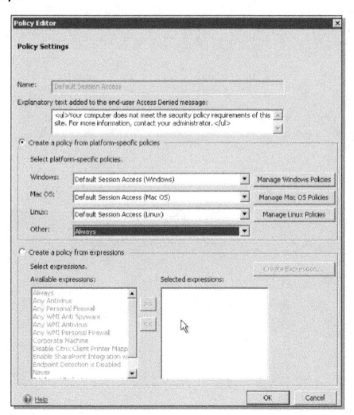

5. We can now close the **Manage Policies and Expressions** screen and select **OK** to return to the UAG management console.

> Selecting **Always** in our access policies for other devices will invariably grant access with no check or with no control to any client not running Windows, Mac OS, or Linux. That is a configuration we have to accept for mobile devices. We will talk more about end point policies in the next section.

6. We have to make the SharePoint application available to mobile devices. We have to select the SharePoint application and select the **Edit...** button:

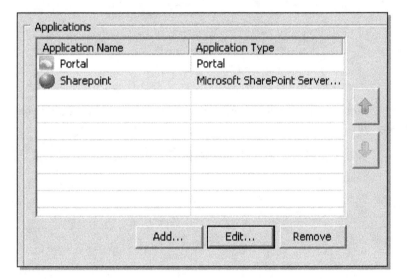

7. In the **Application Properties** dialog box, click on the **Portal Link** tab and check the following options: **Allow rich clients to bypass trunk authentication, Premium Mobile Portal**, and **Non-premium mobile Portal**.

 As we said before, the **Rich clients** option will be very useful to enable the Office Hub integration with mobile devices such as a Windows phone.

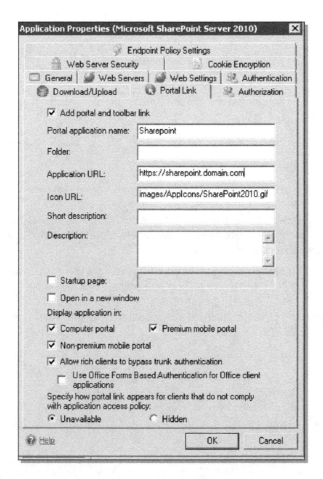

8. The last step to publish SharePoint with UAG is to edit the AAM in SharePoint so that the server is able to answer to the connections arriving from UAG.

9. On the **Alternate Access Mappings** page, in the **Alternate Access Mapping Collection** list, click on **Change Alternate Access Mapping Collection**, and then on the **Select an Alternate Access Mapping Collection** dialog box, select the SharePoint application that we want to publish.

On the **Alternate Access Mappings** page, click on **Edit Public URLs**.

In the following screenshot, we have added the URL we used to configure the trunk in UAG:

 Here we have to enter the same public hostname that we used in the **Public host name** box when we added the SharePoint web application to the trunk.

It is really important that the URL includes the protocol (HTTP or HTTPS), and that it is the same as the trunk type.

10. Now opening the UAG portal from a mobile device (a Windows phone, for instance), we are able to launch SharePoint:

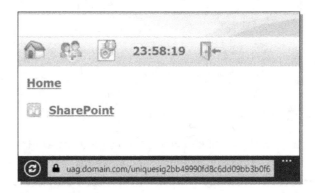

11. We will be redirected to the mobile version of our SharePoint application. Please note that our user does not need to remember the URL of the SharePoint server, because the starting point is inside the UAG portal.

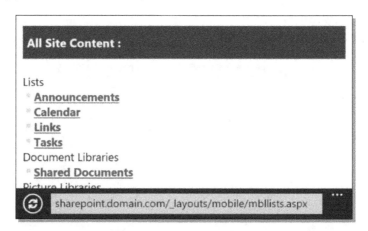

SharePoint Workspace Mobile

SharePoint Workspace Mobile is part of Office Mobile (so on a Windows phone we do not have to download or install anything) and it allows users to open, edit, and synchronize Office documents with SharePoint servers. If our organization uses UAG, we are able to take advantage of the mobile features from any place with a working Internet connection. We have to check an additional configuration of UAG, to be sure that it will work with Office Mobile, so click on the **Configure** button in the **Configure Trunk Settings** zone.

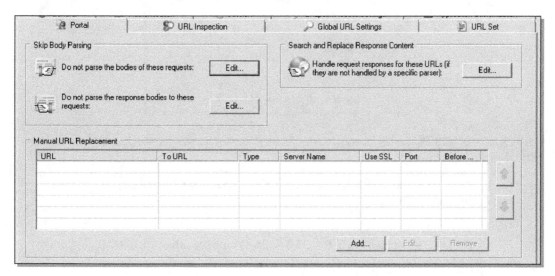

From the **Portal** tab, we have to click on the **Edit...** button for **Do not parse the response bodies to these requests**. In the **Server** list we should find the SharePoint host that we configured in previous steps with the following URLs in the list:

+ .*/_vti_bin/webs\.asmx

+ .*/_vti_bin/lists\.asmx

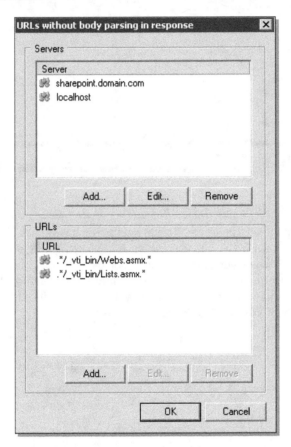

The steps to configure the connection to our SharePoint server from a Windows Phone Version 7.5 are given as follows:

1. In the **Start menu**, flick left to the app list, and navigate to **Settings | Applications | Office**.

2. Tap the UAG server.

3. On the UAG server screen, in the UAG address box, type the URL of UAG, beginning with `https://`.

4. In the **User name** box, type the domain account information and password.

5. Tap **Done**.

Now we have to configure our SharePoint site using the following steps:

1. On **Start**, flick left to the app list, and then tap on **Office**.
2. Flick to **Locations**, and then tap on **SharePoint**.
3. Next to **https://**, type the URL for a SharePoint site.
4. We are now ready to work with the SharePoint contents.

Top features you need to know about

During the previous sections, we configured UAG from scratch and gained experience with application publishing in UAG.

In this section, we will take a quick look at some of the most interesting and necessary features.

To ease the reading of the various topics, we are splitting them into three fields:

+ Most common application publishing scenarios
+ Security and customization
+ Monitoring, maintaining, and troubleshooting

 A deep dive in topics such as customization or security is out of our scope, so please consider the explanations here only as a helpful first step into a broader world.

Most common application publishing scenarios

If we are going to deploy UAG in a mobility scenario, it is almost certain that we will be asked to publish at least one of the following applications: ActiveSync, Dynamics CRM, or Lync (SharePoint for sure is in the list, but that is something we have already talked about).

Publishing Exchange ActiveSync for mobile devices

UAG offers, by default, three ways to access Exchange: Outlook Web Access, Exchange ActiveSync, and Outlook Anywhere. ActiveSync is the instrument for mobile users to synchronize their exchange e-mail messages, calendar information, contact, task data, and so on; that is why we are especially interested in it. Similarly, UAG authenticates the user and then enables access to the Exchange information, giving us an additional security layer between the Internet and the Exchange servers.

To publish ActiveSync, we add an application to the trunk the same way we did for SharePoint and we select a **Web** value from the list of applications. Here we have selected **Microsoft Exchange Server (all versions)** from the list:

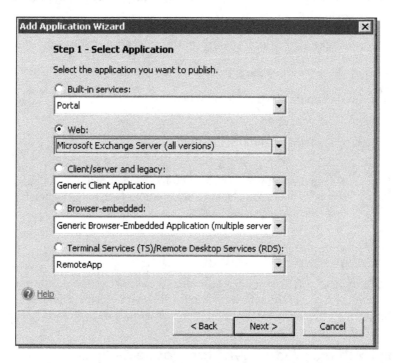

Then we have to select the version of Exchange that we deployed in our environment, and the services we will enable through UAG (in this example we will go with **Exchange ActiveSync** only):

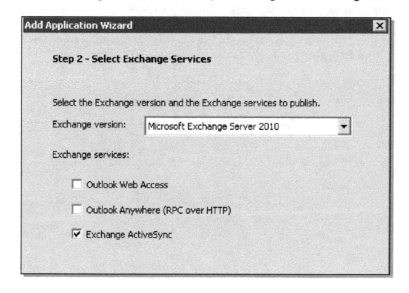

We will be asked for an application name (in our example, `ActSync`), and then we will have to select the end point policies (again, nothing new, it is the same part of the wizard that we have seen before). Depending on the kind of Exchange infrastructure we have, we will select a single server or a farm (we have a single server), and then we are requested to insert the name of our Exchange Server and it will be the internal name of the server, so that we are not exposing the mail services directly to the Internet.

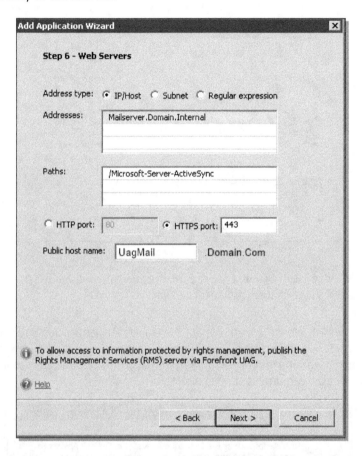

We have the Exchange paths automatically configured by the wizard. The **Public host name** value we are giving is the FQDN that we want to use to publish the Exchange service (pointing it to the public IP of the UAG server).

> The address we use here must be the FQDN of the Exchange server (a CAS server in an Exchange 2007 or 2010 scenario). Using IP addresses will create errors.

The next screen of the wizard will ask for the authentication server. Looking at the following screenshot, we are able to see that there is no free selection of **Authentication Method**, and that **Allow rich clients to bypass trunk authentication** is selected by default with no way of changing the settings:

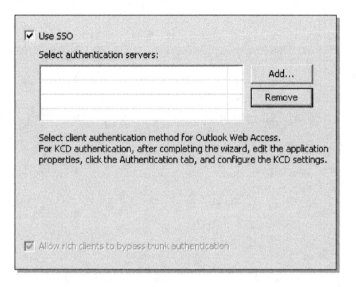

 We will talk more about authentication methods and SSO later in the chapter, as a security topic.

However, the option will allow clients to bypass the trunk's authentication and use basic authentication or NTLM authentication, and that is something we need to use ActiveSync for. We will receive a final warning message stating that rich clients (mobile devices in our scenario) cannot be authenticated through the portal directly.

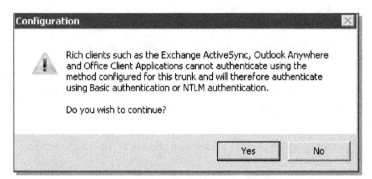

The next screen will give us the opportunity to customize the link on the portal.

 ActiveSync will not create any icon on the portal screen, so that is not a problem indicator.

Next we will have to configure the authorizations and then we will have finished the configuration on the server side.

Application Name	Application Type
Portal	Portal
ActSync	Microsoft Exchange Server ...

The last step is, as usual, to activate the new UAG configuration.

 UAG supports (also) the use of RSA authentication. A security scenario that's interesting for mobile devices is to require mobile users to insert an RSA pin code after the first login to the UAG portal (let's say, to create a second tighter layer of security for a more sensible application). We will talk again about RSA later, but a frequently asked about implementation is to use RSA with UAG publishing ActiveSync. Please remember that the bypass trunk authentication and the way UAG talks with the CAS server makes the RSA solution not a viable one with UAG and mobile devices.

The process to configure ActiveSync on a mobile device varies from client to client and from version to version. In Windows Phone 7.5, for example, we will have to go to **Settings | email+accounts | add an account** with **advanced setup,** and insert the configuration data (we could also go with the Outlook account configuration, again it's a matter of how Exchange is configured in your company).

In our scenario, we will select **Exchange ActiveSync**.

The information required for ActiveSync is the same we use for Exchange, but the server URL is the one we've configured when publishing Exchange ActiveSync (in our example, `UagMail.Domain.Com`).

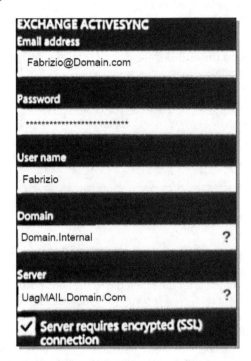

 If we plan to use UAG with Service Pack 2 to sync with Exchange from an Android operating system, read the TechNet article *Release notes for Forefront UAG SP2* available at `http://technet.microsoft.com/en-us/library/jj590881.aspx`.

Publishing Dynamics CRM 2011 for mobile devices

Microsoft Dynamics CRM is a **customer relationship management (CRM)** application supported in an out of the box fashion by UAG. UAG makes it easy to enable external users and partners to use Dynamics, granting a high level of security. Talking about mobile devices, it is important to remember that in UAG SP2, when we publish Dynamics CRM, the console shows the default access, upload, and download end point policies in use, but Dynamics always uses application-specific policies, overriding the end point policy.

For example, a Dynamics CRM application will always use the CRM upload and CRM download policies (and so it is important to configure these policies to work with our mobile devices).

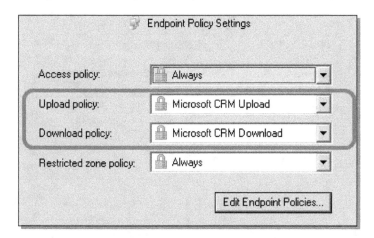

 Also, OWA and SharePoint applications have their specific policies for upload and download, and they are the ones that will be applied (not the default ones).

Publishing Lync for mobile devices

The request to publish Lync using UAG is something we often have (for various reasons). However, the right answer to this request is that UAG is able to publish only the web services of Lync and not Lync Mobility. In addition, the fact that we have TMG running on the same host is absolutely not relevant (that is, we cannot use the TMG deployment of UAG to do the work we have to do with a dedicated server). I suggest reading the entire article *UAG, Lync Mobility and other Lync clients* from Ben Ari's UAG blog to clear any doubts (`http://blogs.technet.com/b/ben/archive/2012/11/09/uag-lync-mobility-and-other-lync-clients.aspx`).

Anyway, for the web services of Lync, there is a dedicated wizard (in the usual **Add Application Wizard**).

After we have added Lync to our portal, we will see three new applications, as shown in the following screenshot:

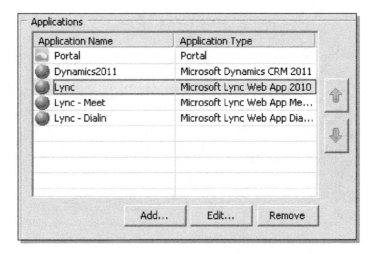

There are also workarounds to publish **Lyncdiscover** that is used from an external network to auto-discover information for mobile clients, and that is not in the list of the applications automatically configured by the wizard. One of the solutions (if we want to configure the aforementioned service in UAG) is *Publish Lync with UAG* (`http://adfordummiez.com/?p=326`), published by *Rune Sørensen*

Security and customization

In the previous part of this section, we used out of the box features and wizards to publish resources (always with heed to mobility). The following topics are all about the internal mechanics of UAG and how they relate to our mobile device's access.

UAG portal selection

UAG uses the user agent string (that each device sends) to select the best portal for the end point (in our situation, as we said previously in the text, the choice is between the Premium mobile portal and the Limited portal). The basic information is in the TechNet article *Customizing the detection module* available at `http://technet.microsoft.com/en-us/library/ff607404.aspx`.

For example, let's try to force Windows Phone 7.5 to use the Limited portal.

 The following modifications are not supported or officially suggested, it is only a way to show how detection works. Please remember to save a copy of the files we are going to edit before making any modifications.

The user agent string is:

```
Mozilla/5.0 (compatible; MSIE 9.0; Windows Phone OS 7.5; Trident/5.0;
IEMobile/9.0; HTC; T8788)
```

One way of reaching the result is to remove the following strings:

```
<DetectionExpression Name="WindowsCE" Expression='Platform Contains
"windows mobile" OR Platform Contains "wince" OR Platform Contains
"windows ce" OR UserAgent Contains "windows phone" OR UserAgent
Contains "windows mobile"' DefaultValue="false" />
<DetectionExpression Name="IE" Expression='Browser Contains "ie" OR
Browser Contains "msie"' DefaultValue="false" />
```

And then we modify `DetectionExpression` dedicated to `LimitedMobile`:

```
<DetectionExpression Name="LimitedMobile" Expression='Browser Contains
"ie" OR Browser Contains "msie"' DefaultValue="false" />
```

As expected, we will have the Limited portal login page (text only) on a device that, by default, is enabled to the Premium mobile portal, as shown in the following screenshot:

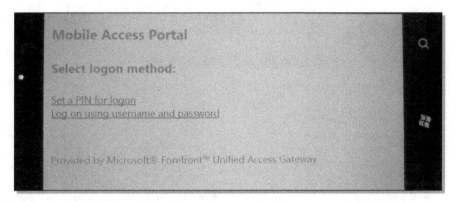

Another way of changing the detection module results is by editing the `mobile.browser` file that contains the definitions of the mobile devices. The previous test will be useful to explore another UAG feature.

PIN logon

The user of a mobile device that is restricted to the Limited portal is offered the opportunity to insert a **Personal Identification Number (PIN)** value.

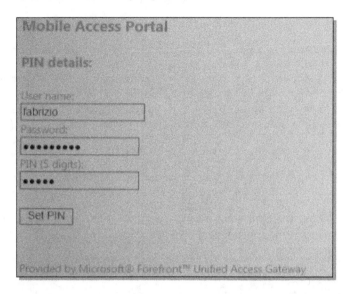

Using the PIN, UAG requires the username and the password only once.

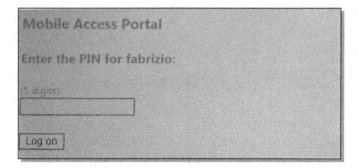

From now on, every time the user tries to access a resource using UAG, he/she is required only to insert the PIN. The idea is to simplify the login phase, thus reducing the number of passwords to type on mobile devices. The PIN system uses encrypted cookies saved on the end point. After the first logon, every time the user tries to access a resource using UAG, the device only sends the cookie that is decrypted on the UAG server. The configuration related to the use of PINs is saved in the config.xml file, located at <UAG path>\von\InternalSite\Mobile\.

UAG portal customization

UAG supports the customization of various elements to keep the user experience in line with our company standards.

 A complete customization of the UAG trunks and applications may be really complex and may also require working with ASP and CSS files (so it's not in the list of the things we will see during this book).

A good starting point, if we want to tailor the portal to our company's identity, is the TechNet article *Customizing the portal* available at `http://technet.microsoft.com/en-us/library/ff607389.aspx`.

The example that will follow uses the `CustomUpdate` mechanism, which is a one-of-a-kind UAG. We can try and populate some folders within the UAG folder structure that are known to contain custom files, and UAG will automatically incorporate them into its code. To give you an idea, the easiest way to replace existing images is to give the custom files the same names as the ones we're going to replace, and put them in the `CustomUpdate` folder (for example, for the login page, `<UAG path>\InternalSite\Images\CustomUpdate`).

This is a way of customizing the UAG look with low risk and low impact on the existing code (to roll back, we simply have to remove the custom contents).

Back to our (simple) customization example; we want a warning message displayed on mobile devices that are requesting access. We will achieve that by applying a modification of the default text.

The easiest way to create custom texts is to edit the XML files located at `<UAG path>\von\InternalSite\Languages\CustomUpdate`.

There are XML files for many languages, for example, users with the English language will read text located in the `en-US.xml` file.

The first screen we have that opens the UAG from a mobile device has a header reading **Application and Network Access Portal**.

So if we want to customize it, we have to copy the `en-US.xml` file in the `CustomUpdate` folder and modify the line reading:

```
<String id="2" _locID="2">Application and Network Access Portal</
String>
```

For example, we could use the following string:

```
<String id="2" _locID="2">Custom Company UAG Portal : Authorized Users
Only</String
```

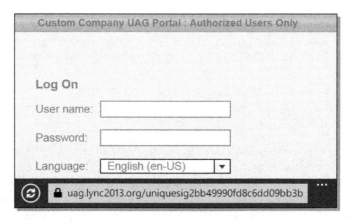

Endpoint detection

A large part of the UAG security is based on a mechanism known as Endpoint Detection. When the user accesses the UAG portal, a series of controls are performed on the client for security and compliance reasons. We are able to manage endpoint access policies at three different levels: **trunk, portal,** and **application** (in the following screenshot, we can have a look of the policies at the **trunk** level):

Every time a client tries to connect, UAG uses the detection component (which is part of the client components) to assess the security status of the client and to trigger policy actions.

The client must install some software components on the local machine (Forefront UAG endpoint components). The issue with mobile devices is that the two versions of the components (ActiveX and Java Applet) are not supported on mobile devices, and so all the clients falling in this category are classified as "Other Devices". The only operation supported is using the device ID (with Microsoft Exchange Server 2010) to limit the use of ActiveSync at the user's mailbox level (and that's not something strictly related to UAG) as explained in the TechNet article *Disable a Mobile Phone for Exchange ActiveSync* at `http://technet.microsoft.com/en-us/library/bb232080.aspx`.

In the *Monitoring, maintaining, and troubleshooting* section we will talk about the endpoint monitoring tools we have in UAG.

 UAG includes policies related to the use of a certified endpoint that may sound extremely interesting in a scenario with mobile devices. Nonetheless, the feature is related to client components not available for mobile clients.

A quick word on Network Access Protection (NAP)

Earlier in the book, when we configured the first trunk, we said that we were able to use UAG access policies or Microsoft **Network Access Protection** (**NAP**).

Now you could be wondering if selecting NAP would be a better solution to enforce endpoint policies. Sadly, the answer is most likely a no. NAP requires a client-side agent and enforcement client that are not available for mobile devices, so the best we could get is to set a generic policy (that's something similar to what we have with UAG policies and is really more complicated).

UAG authentication and SSO

On a mobile device, having to input a password for every application we use is a time-consuming (and error-prone) activity.

UAG helps us in this case because when a client authenticates during the login process to UAG, we are able to delegate authentication and use the same credentials for different applications in the same trunk.

That's something we are able to set, selecting an application in the selected trunk, opening the **Web Settings** tab, and configuring **Use single-sign on to send credentials to published applications**.

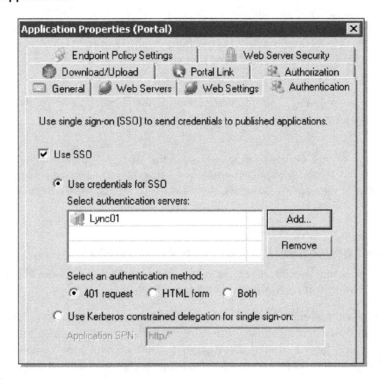

If the published server is using an HTTP-based schema (Basic, NTLM, and Integrated Windows Authentication), we have to use **401 request**. If we have a form-based authentication, activate the **HTML form** radio button. The **Both** selection is to address a scenario in which the two authentication methods are required together. We have already explored **Allow rich clients to bypass trunk authentication**, which is needed for services that cannot authenticate using the trunk's authentication, and that requires a direct basic or NTLM authentication. The last option, **Use Kerberos constrained delegation for single sign-on**, requires the trunk to authenticate using any method, and then UAG will perform the SSO presenting a Kerberos ticket to the backend web application.

Monitoring, maintaining, and troubleshooting

One of the most important activities we have to carry out when managing mobile device interaction with UAG is to troubleshoot the different issues that may arise during the aforementioned intercommunication. It is a really complex argument, so the best we can do right now is to take a quick look at the most important tools we have at our disposal and study them deeper in a moment.

Back up and restore UAG configuration

UAG creates a backup of our configuration when we activate a modification (as we have seen in the previous examples).

 The backup mechanism creates an XML file containing the trunk and application configuration. All the settings related to the operating system have to be saved with one of the many standard backup methods.

By default, the configuration is saved in the `<UAG path>\Backup` folder, and it contains the trunk and application configuration in an XML file. If we want to export or import our configuration manually, we can use the UAG management console and on the **File** menu, select **Export** (or **Import**).

Alternatively, we can use the `ConfigMgr` command (`<UAG path>\utils\ConfigMgr\ConfigMgrUtil.exe`) to export:

```
ConfigMgrUtil Export (-exp) xml_file password [comment]
```

Or to import:

```
ConfigMgrUtil Import (-imp) xml_file password
```

The aforementioned actions are useful also if we want to create additional servers (for a lab environment, for example).

If we want to import a configuration saved from a previous version into an upgraded installation of UAG (for example, for a migration test from UAG SP1 to SP2), we have to modify the following registry key to a value of 1:

```
HKEY_LOCAL_MACHINE\SOFTWARE\WhaleCom\e-Gap\
Configuration\ImportFromOtherVersion
```

Refer to *Backing up and restoring with export and import* available at: `http://technet.microsoft.com/en-us/library/ee406185.aspx`.

Configuration tasks requiring registry modifications

The *Forefront UAG registry keys* TechNet article (`http://technet.microsoft.com/en-us/library/ee809087.aspx`) contains some of the tasks we are able to launch *only* from the registry (like the previous backup and restore operation with unmatched UAG versions)

UAG Web Monitor

The UAG **Web Monitor** is the tool we use to verify information about the activities related to sessions, applications, users, and so on.

It's located in the UAG management console, and it's installed by default.

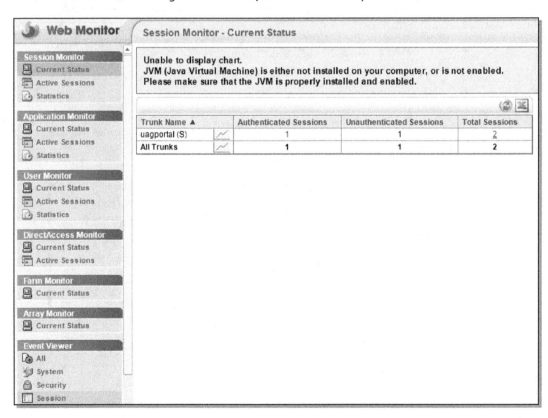

In the UAG **Web Monitor,** we will have data about active sessions, session statistics, server status, reports, and endpoint information (and more). For example, as we said, when talking about endpoint policies, we are able to read information about the client with an Active Session (going to **Session Monitor, Active Sessions**, and selecting the Session ID we want to examine). In the following screenshot we have information about the endpoint:

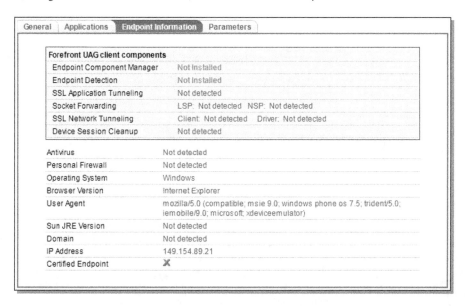

And in the next screenshot we have information about the session parameters (we are using a Windows Phone Emulator):

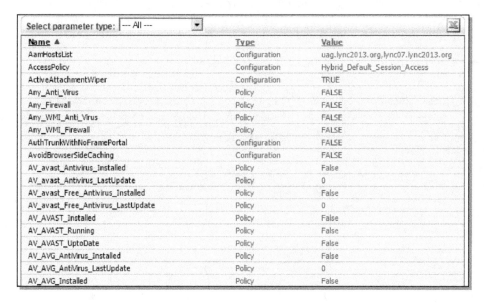

UAG tracing

Standard tools, such as the Web Monitor we talked about previously, often do not provide enough information on errors and events related to UAG. Luckily UAG uses a mechanism known as **Event Tracing for Windows (ETW)** that we are able to configure using a graphical interface `Trace.HTA`.

It's launched using the `LaunchHTA.VBS` script in `<UAG path>\common\bin\tracing`.

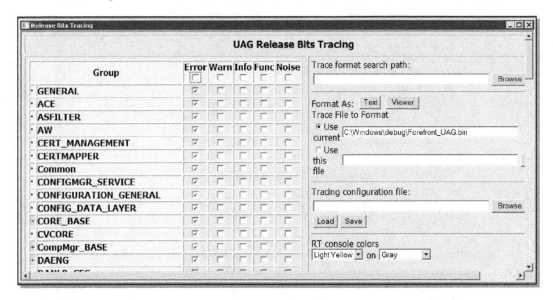

The amount of information registered and managed here is huge, but there are a couple of really good articles about `Trace.HTA` from where we could get started on the use of the tool, first from Ben Ari's UAG and IAG blog (again) and the second one from Frédéric ESNOUF's blog:

- ✦ *UAG Tracing made simple* (`http://blogs.technet.com/b/ben/archive/2010/09/03/uag-tracing-made-simple.aspx`)

- ✦ *Tracing UAG: don't be blind ;-)* (`http://blogs.technet.com/b/fesnouf/archive/2010/03/17/tracing-uag-don-t-be-blind.aspx`)

People and places you should get to know

UAG often requires modifications and workarounds to achieve the level of customization we want for our company.

Here we have a (short) list of sites and people that could be really important to understand UAG and resolve issues.

Official sites

✦ The official homepage of Forefront Unified Access Gateway 2010. It's a great place for information and news about the product:

    http://www.microsoft.com/en-us/server-cloud/forefront/unified-access-gateway.aspx

✦ The official TechNet documentation of UAG:

    http://technet.microsoft.com/en-us/library/ff358694.aspx

✦ The Forefront UAG Product Team blog doesn't have many posts but every one counts:

    http://blogs.technet.com/b/edgeaccessblog/

✦ The Microsoft TechNet Wiki, with a lot of contribution and continuous updates from the Microsoft technical community:

    http://social.technet.microsoft.com/wiki/

Community

✦ TechNet Forums: *Forefront Edge Security – DirectAccess, UAG, and IAG* at http://social.technet.microsoft.com/Forums/en-US/forefrontedgeiag/threadsx

✦ Microsoft Forefront and Cloud Security Forums at http://forums.forefrontsecurity.org/

✦ Microsoft UAG interest group on LinkedIn at http://www.linkedin.com/groups/Microsoft-UAG-interest-group-3727281/about

Blogs

◆ Ben Ari's UAG and IAG blog is a great source of suggestions and tech solutions for UAG (`http://blogs.technet.com/b/ben/`)

◆ Forefront blog from Sander de Wit, Jorn Lutters, and Stefan van der Wiele, where their posts are in depth and well written (`http://www.forefrontblog.nl/`)

◆ The ISA Server blog is focused on ISA but more often UAG has an important role in their writings (`http://blogs.isaserver.org/`)

◆ Richard Hicks' Forefront TMG blog at `http://tmgblog.richardhicks.com/category/forefront-uag-2010/`

Twitter

◆ MS Forefront Team, the official Twitter account for Microsoft's Identity and Security Business: `@MS_Forefront`

◆ *Peter Geelen*, PFE Security and Identity at Microsoft: `@geelenp`

◆ *Dieter Rauscher*, Microsoft Forefront MVP: `@Dieter_Rauscher`

◆ *Lionel Leperlier*, Microsoft Forefront MVP: `@liontux`

◆ *Andres Galvan*, Microsoft Forefront MVP, tweets in Spanish: `@andres_gal`

Thank you for buying
Instant Microsoft Forefront UAG Mobile Configuration Starter

About Packt Publishing

Packt, pronounced 'packed', published its first book "*Mastering phpMyAdmin for Effective MySQL Management*" in April 2004 and subsequently continued to specialize in publishing highly focused books on specific technologies and solutions.

Our books and publications share the experiences of your fellow IT professionals in adapting and customizing today's systems, applications, and frameworks. Our solution based books give you the knowledge and power to customize the software and technologies you're using to get the job done. Packt books are more specific and less general than the IT books you have seen in the past. Our unique business model allows us to bring you more focused information, giving you more of what you need to know, and less of what you don't.

Packt is a modern, yet unique publishing company, which focuses on producing quality, cutting-edge books for communities of developers, administrators, and newbies alike. For more information, please visit our website: www.packtpub.com.

Writing for Packt

We welcome all inquiries from people who are interested in authoring. Book proposals should be sent to author@packtpub.com. If your book idea is still at an early stage and you would like to discuss it first before writing a formal book proposal, contact us; one of our commissioning editors will get in touch with you.

We're not just looking for published authors; if you have strong technical skills but no writing experience, our experienced editors can help you develop a writing career, or simply get some additional reward for your expertise.

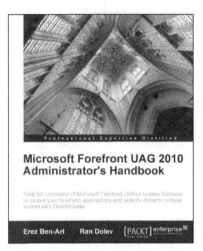

Microsoft Forefront UAG 2010 Administrator's Handbook

ISBN: 978-1-84968-162-9   Paperback: 484 pages

Take full command of Microsoft Forefront Unified Access Gateway to secure your business applications and provide dynamic remote access with DirectAccess

1. Maximize your business results by fully understanding how to plan your UAG integration

2. Consistently be ahead of the game by taking control of your server with backup and advanced monitoring

3. An essential tutorial for new users and a great resource for veterans

PhoneGap Mobile Application Development Cookbook

ISBN: 978-1-84951-858-1   Paperback: 320 pages

Over 40 recipes to create mobile applications using the PhoneGap API with examples and clear instrucitons

1. Use the PhoneGap API to create native mobile applications that work on a wide range of mobile devices

2. Discover the native device features and functions you can access and include within your applications

3. Packed with clear and concise examples to show you how to easily build native mobile applications

Please check **www.PacktPub.com** for information on our titles

Responsive Web Design with HTML5 and CSS3

ISBN: 978-1-84969-318-9   Paperback: 324 pages

Learn responsive design using HTML5 and CSS3 to adapt website to any browser or screen size

1. Everything needed to code websites in HTML5 and CSS3 that are responsive to every device or screen size

2. Learn the main new features of HTML5 and use CSS3's stunning new capabilities including animations, transitions and transformations

3. Real world examples show how to progressively enhance a responsive design while providing fall backs for older browsers

Marmalade SDK Mobile Game Development Essentials

ISBN: 978-1-84969-336-3   Paperback: 318 pages

Get to grips with the Marmalade SDK to develop games for a wide range of mobile devices, including iOS, Androide, and more

1. Easy to follow with lots of tips, examples and diagrams, including a full game project that grows with each chapter

2. Build video games for all popular mobile platforms, from a single codebase, using your existing C++ coding knowledge

3. Master 2D and 3D graphics techniques, including animation of 3D models, to make great looking games

Please check **www.PacktPub.com** for information on our titles

www.ingramcontent.com/pod-product-compliance
Lightning Source LLC
LaVergne TN
LVHW080103070326
832902LV00014B/2395